It's just a memento of the South. Enjoy. Love Julianne xoxo 2003

A Field Guide
to Southern Speech

"FIELD & STREAM [recently] published a sampling of Southern sporting phrases from Charles Nicholson, a very funny writer from Alabama. Now, Nicholson's work has been enlarged and collected in a hilarious new book, *A Field Guide to Southern Speech.*"

DUNCAN BARNES, EDITOR
FIELD & STREAM

A Field Guide to Southern Speech

A Twelve-Gauge Lexicon for the Duck Blind, the Deer Stand, the Skeet Shoot, the Bass Boat, and the Backyard Barbecue

Charles Nicholson

August House / Little Rock

PUBLISHERS

Printed in the United States of America

10 9 8 7 6

LIBRARY OF CONGRESS CATALOGING-IN-PUBLICATION DATA

Nicholson, Charles, 1946-
A field guide to Southern speech: a twenty-gauge lexicon for the
duck blind, the deer stand, the skeet shoot, the bass boat, and the
backyard barbecue/Charles Nicholson.—1st ed.
p. cm.
ISBN 0-87483-098-2 (alk. paper)
1. English language—Provincialisms—Southern States—Glossaries,
vocabularies, etc.
2. Americanisms—Southern States—Dictionaries.
3. Southern States—Popular culture—Miscellanea. I. Title.
PE2926.N53 1989   89-14872
427' .975—dc20   CIP

Cover design by Byron Taylor
Illustrations by Wendell E. Hall
Production artwork by Ira Hocut
Typography by Lettergraphics, Memphis, Tennessee
Design direction by Ted Parkhurst
Project direction by Hope Coulter

Portions of this manuscript originally appeared in *Field and Stream*
(January 1988).

This book is printed on archival-quality paper which meets the
guidelines for performance and durability of the Committee on
Production Guidelines for Book Longevity of the Council on
Library Resources.

AUGUST HOUSE, INC.   PUBLISHERS   LITTLE ROCK

Gone with the Ducks

It is a well-kept but nevertheless apocryphal secret that the American Civil War actually started because of a misunderstanding between two duck-hunters, a Southerner named Jefferson D. Beauregard IV and his Yankee father-in-law, one Abraham Oldsmobile.

It happened in the early morning hours of the twelfth of April, 1861 (there being no official duck season that year, and even fewer game wardens), when Young Jeff and Old Abe were hiding in some cattails near the mouth of Charleston Harbor. Old Abe complained about the location, urging his son-in-law to move the boat nearer to what Abe believed to be the ducks' natural flyway.

"You've got good eyes, Jeff. But I don't believe"—Abe began, but because Jeff had put a bit too much mint in his juleps the night before, only this last part of the sentence reached his brain: "I can see ducks so far away."

Immediately alert at the mention of game, Jeff looked high and low for ducks, to no avail. But being a true Southern Gentleman and therefore wishing to avoid even the appearance of insult to his wife's father, Yankee or not, Jeff raised his gun to his shoulder, pointed it toward the dark and empty pre-dawn sky, and fard away.

His mistake would have been harmless, had not the Confederates at Fort Johnson, on hearing the loud retort from Jeff's big ten-gauge echoing across the harbor, erroneously assumed they were being attacked by the Yankees at Fort Sumter and returned far. This not only started the War Between the States, but scared the ducks so bad it ruined the hunting around Charleston for nearly a week.

So now if somebody catches you reading this book, all you have to do is tell them that story and then explain how three Southern Gentlemen spent twenty grueling years under actual field conditions putting together this collection of words that Yankees say wrong, and that we did it just so there won't be any more wars.

Then, if they believe that, you tell 'em that me and Bubba and Elrod are getting up a snipe hunt down in the river swamp tonight and all of yawl are invited, Yankee or not!

stood: laid down. "We could have stood in bed and caught as many fish as we did today."

pier: seem. "That don't pier to be a buck."

dade: deceased. "Go over and poke that bear to see is he dade or just asleep."

tuck: past tense of *take*. "The feller that sold me this waterbed sleeping bag sure tuck me in."

fanger: one of the digits of the hand. "Always pick your nose with your thumb when you're hunting, Elrod. That way you won't get no boogers stuck on your trigger fanger."

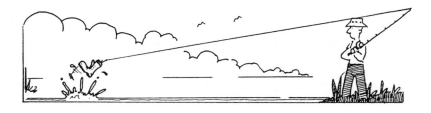

rat: opposite of *lef.*

paradise: gambling paraphernalia. "The crap game broke up after the boy who had the paradise lost."

chittlins: Southern epicurean indelicacy whose ignobility of origin is surpassed only by the lowly mountain oyster.

keel: to inflict grievous bodily harm, even unto death.

ketch: 1. snatch a ball from the air   2. surprise in an illicit act.

yawl: second person plural pronoun. Possessive: yawls. There is no singular. "I'll keel yawl if I ever ketch yawl messing with my sailboat again."

siddown: what most folks do on a deer stand.

see: what you try to do in a blind.

duck down: what you have to do in a duck blind (see "see").

this year: not that thar.

smother: not this year.

line: what outdoorsmen are often accused of. "Elmer says he caught a ten-pound bass in this lake, but I believe he's line."

lilac: the correlation of prevarication. "Ever time we start talking about fishing allst Bubba can do is lilac a rug."

mast: something people wear on their faces and trees wear on their limbs. "Leroy says he can hunt better with a camouflaged mast, so I made me one out of acorns and pine cones."

labber doe: type of hunting dog. "Them labber doe retrievers is good for fetching back ducks."

Miss Sippy: the biggest river in the South.

Lucy Anna: a "sportsman's paradise," thanks partly to the Miss Sippy.

onliest: superlative of only. Note: Several Southern words ending in *-t* and *-st* have been omitted from most Yankee dictionaries. Besides *onliest*, these include *allst, bestest, lastest, mostest, chanst, wisht,* and *ast.*

bipt overhauls: long-necked blue jeans.

attar: wearing apparel. "Beulah says I cain't wear my bipt overhauls to the fish fry because it ain't proper attar for a man of my statute and swaiver far."

prince: animal tracks. "Don't worry, that's just a big dawg's prince. There ain't been a bear in these parts for years."

crick: small stream. "My Uncle Junior said he twisted his neck when he fell in the crick."

oncet: half of twicet.

waller: behave uncouthly. "Yawl cain't waller with the hawgs all night and spect to soar with the eagles in the mawnin."

ATV: one television, which many Southern outdoorsmen think is one too many.

rurnt: 1. beyond repair   2. extremely intoxicated   3. both.

trawl: small ogre. "Turn the boat so we won't drag our lines under that old bridge, Elrod. It looks lack a bad place for a trawl."

deliver: what some folks consider de best part of de deer.

hat trick: the only way to get a Southern outdoorsman to remove his hat. "I only take my hat off for three thangs, and this year ain't one of 'em."

poultry: rhythmic, often rhyming verse.

Load Tennisshoe: Victorian poet whose popularity among English teachers has long been the bane of young Southern outdoorsmen. "I cain't go coon hunting tonight. I got to stay home and memorize some poultry by that Alfred, Load Tennisshoe."

bout: almost. "Yawl bout ready to head back to camp?"

doohickey: anything you don't know the proper name for. "Hand me that doohickey and hold still, Elrod. I get ticks off my dawg this way all the time."

stoont: pupil. "When Beulah started back to college she ast the teacher was she the oldest stoont they had. He said no, but he believed she was the two ugliest."

hind foot: invisible appendage found only on Southern mothers who are especially sensitive to prevarication. "Finished your homework my hind foot! You put that fishing pole down rat now."

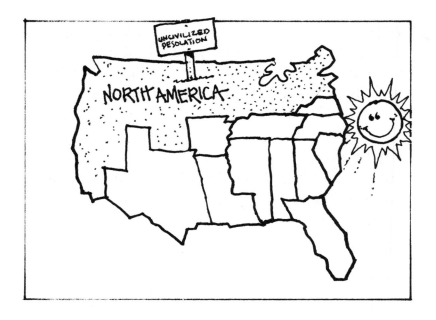

North America: the uncivilized area north
of Mr. Mason's and Mr. Dixon's line, plus all of
California.

South America: Alabama, Arkansas, Florida, Georgia, Louisiana, Mississippi, North Carolina, South Carolina, Tennessee, Texas, and
Virginia.

idjit: a person who is smarter than a mowron but can't prove it. "I bet I looked lack a idjit sitting there in the doctor's office with that fish hook and all them worms hanging out my nose."

hat: anything a Southerner puts on his head that won't bite.

cap: what you shoot in a toy gun.

castes: plural of *cast*. "That Bubba cain't make three castes without getting a backlash."

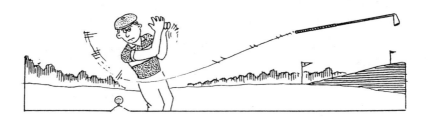

bay net: long, sharp knife. "Somebody ought to tell Bubba he's supposed to take that bay net off his raffle afore he eats his peas with it."

hah sherf: top law enforcement official. "Put these extra fish under your hat and try to act natural, Elrod. Yonder comes the game warden and the hah sherf both."

fern: not domestic. "My Uncle Junior's been hunting in New Mexico and a whole bunch of other fern countries."

cumanup: approaching. "Looks like there's a storm cumanup on the other side of the lake."

arnge: 1. round, juicy fruit from Florida   2. safety color for hunting attire. "Deers is all colorblind, Elrod, so hunter arnge is just a pigment of their imagination."

bub what quell: popular game bird. "That Yankee says he's used to hunting ptarmigans and ruffled grouses, but I don't believe he knows a mawnin dove from a bub what quell."

ptarmigan: Yankee game bird impossible to pronounce.

windshield factor: scientific value which combines speed and temperature to tell you how cold it will feel when you stick your head out from behind the windshield.

tamar: the day after today.

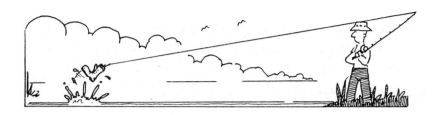

quawtah: one-fourth. "If than animal is a quawtah hoss, what do the rest of him be?"

tame: use gunsights. "Yawl shooting wild because you don't take time tame."

catfish: bottom-dwelling scavengers remarkably similar to some Southern politicians, being all mouth and no brains.

sexist: a term Southern women sometimes use to describe outdoorsmen. "Load, Ginger. Ain't that Bubba just the sexist thang you ever did see?"

mow drawl: lubricant for internal combustion engines. "Elmer's old truck was burning so much mow drawl he got arrested for cropdusting without a license."

Joyjuh: the peach state. "I here there's some mighty fine quell hunting down in south Joyjuh."

Joyjuh roadmaps: irrefutable evidence of recent overindulgence. "Load, Elrod, what you been dranking? Your eyes look lack two roadmaps of Joyjuh."

goozle pap: esophagus. "Ever time my Uncle Junior takes a drink of licker his goozle pap wiggles lack a hootchiekootchie dancer."

achoo: used to identify a buddy in the woods. "Hey Joe, achoo?"

nairn: plural of *none.* "We seen bunches of deer, but we didn't shoot nairn."

puhcons: Southern nuts; often mispronounced by Northerners. "That Yankee ast me where he could buy some peacans, but I told him ain't nobody sold slop jars around here for two-three years."

varse: little invisible bug that can make you sick.

hacker: walking enthusiast. "I don't see how a hacker can cause a varse. Allst I ever got was Alf Leak's foot."

far tire: forest ranger's headquarters.

bass ackards: having one's cart before one's horse. "I told Leroy to take the boat out of the water and then pull the drain plug, but that mowron did it bass ackards."

treen wawker: type of hunting dog. "Old Beauregard's mama was a treen wawker and his daddy come from a good neighborhood."

possum: a Southern game animal which must be properly prepared to be appreciated: Scrape the hide, being sure to remove all tire marks; stuff with foil-wrapped potatoes; and bake at 400 degrees for one and one-half hours. Serve potatoes with butter or sour cream. Give the possum to your dogs.

armadillo: possum on the half-shell. Remove shell with hatchet or chainsaw, then prepare as you would possum. Beware of dogs.

probate: tournament-winning lures. Also where you can wind up if you spend all your your money on probate.

spar tar: extra wheel, used when you have a flat or as a flower planter in the front yard. Planters should be painted white unless you have fake flamingoes, in which case either hot pink or chartreuse is acceptable.

eye deer: thought or notion. "Do yawl have any eye deer where the spar tar is on this moder sickle?"

ain't: 1. contraction of *are* and *not*. "I ain't going hunting tonight." 2. your uncle's wife.

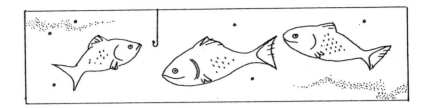

cain't: contraction of *can* and *ain't.* "It ain't that cain't cain't mean you ain't, Elrod, or that ain't cain't mean you cain't. One is when you just are not and the other is when you can but you are not anyway, which is cain't, ain't it?"

hammer road: painful affliction of the der-rière. "Don't say nothing to Uncle Junior about him riding his mule sidesaddle. He says he's got him a hammer road as big as a puhcon and he'll fat the first one that laughs."

dreckly: soon. "We'll be to the lake dreckly."

ladder: fat pine which is extremely flammable and used to make two things, kindling and dynamite. "I know it's cold in here, Elrod, but just throw that whole ladder stump on the far and we'll be burning up in no time."

Great Lakes: There is Chickamauga, Sidney Lanier, Talquin, Guntersville, Pontchartrain, and a whole bunch of other great lakes in the South.

safari: a measure of great distance. "He casted that new probate of his safari bout lost it."

minnow: a state of negative being. "I minnow hurry."

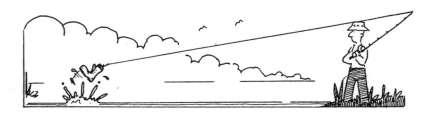

naff: instrument for cutting. "I keep my hunting naff so sharp that when I shave with it I don't get five o'clock shadow till half past eight."

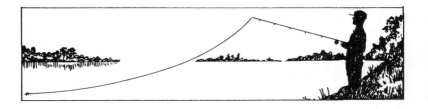

slud: past tense of *slad*. "When I slipped and started to slad down the mountainsad, I just saddown and slud."

tarnayshun: the whole country. "Sears the best bass lake in the tarnayshun."

force: bunch of trees. "I didn't understand that movie, Elrod. How can the force be with them if there ain't so much as a hackberry bush up there in outdoor space?"

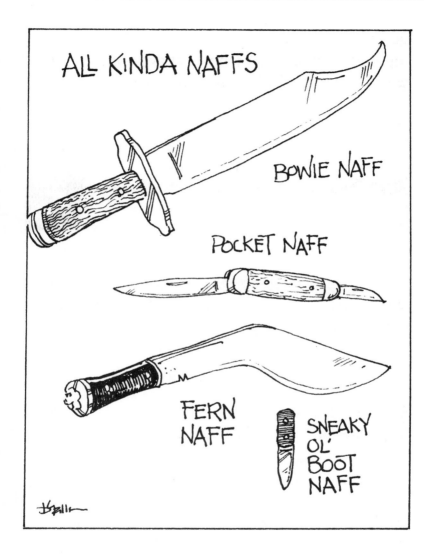

in hurt: receive as a bequest. "I thought I was gonna in hurt Grampaw's shotgun, but allst he left me was a broke pocketnaff with half a pitcher of Elvis on the handle."

poke rand: type of fish bait. "You reckon they call them big bass 'hawgs' because of the way they lack poke rand?"

poke salat: green, leafy vegetable found throughout the South. Often mistakenly called poke salad, which as any true Southerner knows is cole slaw served with poke barbecue.

downt: toward a specific location.

hard on: given employment. "Elmer's been taking one of them mail-order taxidermy courses so he can get hard on downt the cab company."

fly fishing: No one in the South fishes for flies.

sarmash: main ingredient of the mint julep. "I heard there's gonn be a tax on sarmash whiskey. Reckon it's them prohibitionists again, or just the revenooers?"

moment: additional garnish. "I believe this julep could use a little moment, don't yawl?"

Dook: famous movie star who was made an honorary Southerner because he played Davy Crockett so well—this despite persistent rumors that he once played a Yankee soldier early in his career. "Don't you wish they'd made a movie with the Dook playing GenulLee?"

sunny beaches: what you might call fishermen who beat you to your favorite bass hole.

bass hole: what it sounds like those sunny beaches are calling you.

news: "If you keep tryin to beat me to my fishing hole, me news gonna hafta fat."

cawfee: dark, aromatic beverage usually served hot.

ass cream: milk-based frozen dessert. "Only two thangs I don't lack is yaller waddermillon and cawfee ass cream."

diary: affliction sometimes known as the Green Apple Quick Step.

harmony: cash for the beauty parlor. "Maybellene's gonna be hard to get along with when she finds out we spent her harmony on beer and probate."

green slime: algae growth found on the surface of many Southern lakes and ponds. Also boiled okra. Both are inedible.

Crebble Hook: large, green, man-like creature occasionally sighted in Southern swamps. "I seen on TV how that little feller turns hisself into the Crebble Hook, but reckon what that Abdominal Snowman do?"

stunt show: retard. "Don't shoo know smoking will stunt show growth?"

CREBBLE HOOK

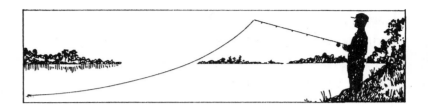

hoe sale: below retail. "My Uncle Junior's a culler downt the worm farm. He lets me have the rejects hoe sale."

share a rain: deluge. "That mowron's still fishing, Elrod. I reckon he ain't got sense enough to get in out of a share a rain."

arsh sitter: type of hunting dog. "That arsh sitter I bought is purty but he ain't too smart. Last week he tried to point the weather vane and fell off the barn."

inside straight: unbeatable poker hand, sometimes referred to as a "Dixie boxing glove." Consists of any five cards in one hand and a straight razor in the other.

toe up: extremely upset, overwrought.

past: 1. completed a grade in school 2. died. "Mama was toe up when my Uncle Junior past. Says she cain't stand to see him just laying there lack that, now he's not in school anymore."

snuff: when you've caught the limit. "I believe that snuff."

fatback: football position made famous by star Southeastern Conference linebacker Huber B. "Hawgbutt" Simpson.

snelled hook: specially prepared fishing hook. "I bought us some snelled hooks, Elrod, but I still don't see how we're supposed to get these snells to stay on unless we take their shales off."

far off: clear up. "I wish it would far off so we could go outside. I'm bout to get cabinet fever."

tar doubt: exhausted. "It was nice of Bubba to loan us his pop-up camper, but by the time we'd toted it to the top of the mountain we was too tar doubt to hunt."

make: become. "James Otis's youngest girl wants to make a game warden, but he thinks she's too skinny."

critter size: find fault. "I'm not one to critter size another man's shooting, but that Bubba couldn't hit the ground with his hat."

vee hickul: mode of transportation. "My Uncle Junior made hisself a pickup truck out of a 1953 Cadillac hearse: only vee hickul I ever saw with a horn that plays 'Shall We Gather at the River' and a slide-out tackle box six feet long."

tara: extreme fear. "That poor Miss Scarlett had to live in Tara till Rhett Butler come to save her."

otter magic: type of gun. "Leroy says his new otter magic shoots so fast he can miss three times now as quick as he used to could just miss twicet."

flow: the bottom of a room or enclosure.

foe in the flow: type of transmission. "My old truck had a otter magic, but this year's got a foe in the flow."

fought: responsibility. "It ain't my fought that campfar's making you choke, Beulah. Everbody knows that smoke follows ugly."

howsuminnyever: an unknown quantity. "The chittlins is all gone, but yawl can eat howsuminnyever mountain oysters you want."

lack: 1. similar to. "We used to have a pickup truck just lack yawls only different." 2. be fond of. "I lack Ack, and Tina too."

stars: penetrating looks. "Turn that flounder over, Elrod. I cain't stand the way them google eyes stars at me."

burr: popular beverage. "Don't talk to that new Yankee barber whilst he's working, Elrod. When I told him I'd lack to get me some burr and go fishing, he cut all my har off."

raffle: type of gun. "I kilt that bear with my new raffle."

genullee: 1. usually.   2. famous Southern war hero. "It is genullee accepted that GenulLee was most often sober, whereas GenulGrant was genullee drunk."

hottern: a measure of relative warmth.

"Sprang is sprung,
Fall is fayul.
Summer is here,
And it's hottern hayul."

buck nekkid: attired in one's birthday suit.
"We tumped over the outhouse and thar sit
Grandpaw, buck nekkid and mad as a wet
hawnit."

minner paws: the change of life. "Beulah
says her mama's moustache is caused by minner
paws, but that sounds fishy to me."

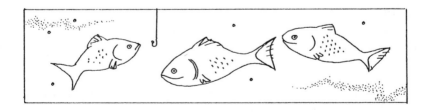

hickernut: common Southern hardwood. "Let's stand under that big hickernut tree till the storm passes, Elrod. Lightning cain't strike it again today."

rain carnation: rebirth after death. "That big old catfish looks just lack the pitcher of my great-great-granddaddy. Do you reckon it's rain carnation, or just fambly resemblance?"

hibachi: a greeting. "Hibachi, Joe. Been doing awrat?"

fidna: about to. "Them barges ain't fidna hit us, Elrod. We got the right of way."

whump-sssss: disturbing sound heard only on two occasions, when a tire blows out, or when a snake falls from overhanging brush into a boat. "Unless this canoe just had a flat tar, me news in deep dookey."

bode: suffix referring to the transom of a boat. "What kind of motor do you lack, inbode or outbode?"

sane: proverb. "My Uncle Junior told me that ever time he loses a fish or misses a shot he just remembers that old sane, 'Never counts your chickens before they cross the road.'"

chill wrens: young humans.

sorta risin: a boil or swollen, infected wound. "I'm gonna have to stand up in the boat today, Elrod. Some far aints got into the outhouse and my whole hind end is sorta risin."

banker merry card: plastic money. "Reckon do this bootlegger take Banker Merry Card?"

natcrollers: long earthworms used for fish bait. "Bubba Junior's lost some of his natcrollers again, so be sure to let him know do any of that basketti you're eating wiggle."

waspers: large stinging insects.

hawnits: larger stinging insects. "Is that a wasper or a hawnit just crawled down your shirt, Elrod?"

tollable: not any better than just okay. "Beulah's squirrel and dumplings is tollable, but her fried coon with blackeye gravy is the best you ever ate."

crawdad: correct pronunciation of *crayfish*.

four-by-four: used in off-road travel. Made by nailing two long two-by-fours together. Very useful when prying trucks out of mudholes. Can also be positioned between lowered tailgate and tree stump to serve as emergency latrine (see "diary").

hit: third person singular pronoun. "Hit don't matter if we hunt here. Old Man Buford just puts them signs up to keep poachers out."

non compass mentis: one who is mentally incapable of using a compass.

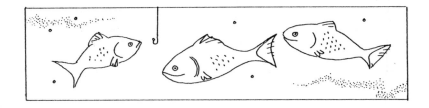

coat odor: a judicial decree. "Bubba's first wife tried to get a coat odor sane he was non compass mentis, but the judge said allst was wrong with that boy was that he lacked direction."

see can you: attempt to. "See can you hit that hawnit's nest with this rock."

sammidge: a lunchtime favorite of Southern outdoorsmen. "I ain't eating road kills, Elrod. Bubba sat on my sammidge."

braid: what you make a sammidge with.

hep: assistance. "Yawl hep me eat up these collards and possum gizzards we had left over from breakfast."

hayul: the unhappy hunting ground. "Beulah told me I'm going to hayul if I don't quit cussing and dranking and laying out with them dawgs all night, so I ast her did she want me to look up any of her kinfolks when I got thar."

boy: any Southern male under the age of sixty-five who is not otherwise qualified to be called "Old Man."

old man: any Southern male who is (1) over sixty-five; (2) a high school principal; or (3) rich. (Note: There has never been a documented case of anyone's being all three.)

skint: removed the hide. "Your wife won't mind that we skint this deer on her dining room table. My ex never did."

bar stool: what Daniel Boone stepped in.

Fat Narsh: Yankee football team that wears gold helmets and sometimes plays against real (i.e., Southern) opponents. "I believe that Alabama Crimson Tad's gonna beat them Fat Narsh next year."

divan: wonderful. "This poke barbecue is divan."

sea gar: large tobacco product for smoking.

bligernt: quarrelsome. "I'm sorry my sea gar burnt a hole in your new down coat, Elrod, but if you'll quit acting so bligernt I'll see can I stick some of these little bitty feathers back in."

sea gulls: observe women.

peckerwood: 1. red-headed bird   2. smart-aleck human. "If that peckerwood says 'I told you so' one more time he can just get this tree off the tent his own self."

par: a source of energy. "You think 800 horse par is too much for a twelve-foot bass boat?"

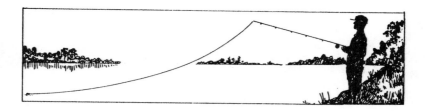

agin: opposed to. "Beluah said the new preacher is agin hunting on Sunday, but I told her that was okay as I hadn't figured on asking him to go anyway."

forum: not aginum.

flardy: 1. bright print fabrics   2. the South-ernmost state in South America. "Have yawl ever noticed how them Flardy folks always wear all them flardy clothes?"

groundhawg: correct name for the animal Yankees call "woodchuck."

yearn: not mine.

summer: used when discussing an indefinite amount. "These rabbits ain't all mine. Summer yearn."

hire: opposite of *lore.*

burried: flying animal. "How many burrieds yawl keel?"

moxican: 1. poisonous snake   2. Indian shoe.

skeer: an unsettling experience. "That old moxican sure gave me a skeer."

paramour: sporting term often heard around Southern hunting and fishing camps. "Annie up, boys. It take a paramour to open, and one-eyed jacks is wild."

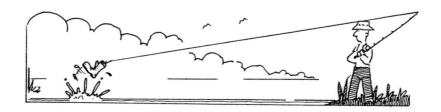

dub barl: type of shotgun. "I wouldn't trade my old dub barl for all the otter magics in the world."

fur: distant. "A shotgun won't shoot fur, but a raffle will."

sturp: the part of the saddle where you put your foot. "When Bubba climbed into the saddle the sturp broke and the mule blowed, but the far didn't start till Elrod lit his sea gar."

hawg: the three-pound bass you caught.

panfish: the seven-pound bass your buddy caught.

two may toes: nutritious vegetable. "My Uncle Junior ordered a BLT at a Yankee truck stop oncet. He said they made it with bacon instead of baloney and sliced the two may toes so thin you could read a newspaper through them."

brars: sticker bushes. "Picking blackberries is fun, except for the chiggers and snakes and waspers and brars."

berl: interment. "When Bubba's old hound dawg Buckshot past they just let fambly come to the funerl, but everbody was invited to the berl."

pyonder: in the sky. "See all them doves pyonder?"

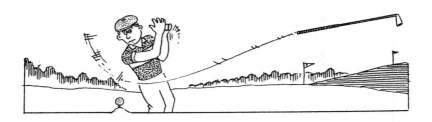

cammer: instrument which produces photographs. "I bought me one of them fish-eyed, whydangle lenses for my cammer so I could get Beulah and her mama both in the same pitcher."

spack: a deer with small antlers.

muley head: an antlerless deer. "We didn't see anything all day but muley heads and spacks."

rockin cheer hat rack: unbelievably large deer antlers. "Elrod, Bubba—would yawl look at the size of the rockin cheer hat rack on that buck! I believe the man who kilt that deer is a liar."

murder: the unfortunate end of many an outdoorsman's career. "Beulah's been trying to make me give up hunting and fishing ever since I murder and mader my waff."

peasant: common derogatory Southern epithet. Pronounced "pissaint."

afore: prior to. "I told yawl to move them fishing poles afore you shut the door."

hominy: a question of quantity. "Hominy fish yawl ketch?" A specific note of caution here: This word is sometimes used in reference to weird-looking corn imported from Yankee land. Southerners use this term in relation to grits only when discussing hominy grits they want for breakfast.

stern: agitating. "Them dawgs is sure stern up them rabbits."

mawnin: the early part of the day. "Good mawnin, Elrod. Did you sleep good after we got the tent back up?"

hay: 1. cow food   2. hello.

unaware: clothing worn next to the skin. "Beulah got me some of that new camouflage unaware so I won't get cold on the snipe hunt."

memo: a question of recall. "How many a yawl memo Ugly McCaslin, the one had buck teeth and won the Mr. Potato Head look-alack contest?"

whup: beat, as in a fight.

bofus: me, and you too. "Bubba ain't gonna want to hear about no accident. When he finds out we're the ones shot the head off his deer decoy he's gonna whup bofus."

gonax: used to express the intention to inquire. "When we get back I'm gonax that boy at the hardware store did he know when he sold it to me that it takes three men to set up this two-man tent."

lat bub: a source of illumination. "Yawl hold this lat bub, Elrod, whilst me and Bubba turns the ladder."

hone: common chore which should be completed before embarking on a hunting or fishing trip. "We can head for the lake as soon as I finish hone these peas."

harass: cereal grain cooked by a female. "I don't know what Beulah's so mad about. Allst I said was we was hungry and she better hurry up and get harass out here, and har gravy and meatloaf too."

no-see-ums: do not exist in the South. Here they grow big and you do-see-um.

stawk: hunting method. "Only thang I don't lack about stawk hunting is you cain't use dawgs."

far: shoot. "Don't far your raffle till you get rat up on that old buck."

fard: past tense of *far.* "If anybody asts who fard that shot, tell 'em I fard it."

blowed: what you thought "fard it" meant.

buckle: often heard in pre-hunt discussions. "There ain't no telling what that buckle do."

field rest: when you have taken the time to remove the guts from freshly killed game. "Did you see how fast I field rest that deer?"

art: okay. "Reckon it'd be art if we painted James Otis's new pickup truck camouflage?"

noon: not an old one.

sears: this is. "That reel's wore out, but sears a noon."

take air: have a family resemblance. "That Bubba Junior sure is smart. He don't take air Bubba atall."

going to streams: showing excessive zeal. "I lack to fish as much as anybody, but I don't believe in going to streams."

hyar: not thar.

guff: a large body of salt water with land on three sides. "My Uncle Junior told me we ought to take our own bait with us when we go fishing downt the Guff. Says you can dig in that white dirt all day long without finding so much as one red wiggler."

spoor: a condition often associated with a lack of funds. "I'd get me one of them new bass boats if I wasn't spoor."

stud: remained erect. "Elmer's first wife Mortiss was so bowlegged and he's so knock-kneed that ever time they stud side by side they spelled 'OX.'"

damyankee: the only kind there is, suh. The only kind there is.

narrow: ammunition for a bonarrow.

warsh: clean with soap and water.

hunting paints: special trousers. "Beulah says she's gonna leave me if I don't warsh my hunting paints this year."

big spenders: what you use to hold your hunting paints up.

poach: open room attached to a house. "Do you want this warshing machine on the front poach or the back poach?"

latter cur: the person who brings the mail. "Old Beauregard's bit the latter cur so many times that allst he'll do now is throw the mail at the gate when he runs by."

strack: when a fish takes your bait.

poppatoom: what you do when you get a strack.

ars: 1. second person plural possessive pronoun 2. units of time. "I believe that boy of ars would hunt twenty-foe ars a day if we'd let him."

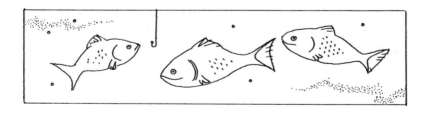

Rusher: the Soviet Union. "My Uncle Junior ate some caviar oncet. Said it was real expensive on account of the onliest place you can get it is from some doctors over in Rusher."

commonist: low-grade people. "That Maybelle thinks her boy Purvis is too good to go possum hunting with the rest of us, but I know for a fact that all her people is just the commonist sort."

compost heap: new name some Yankees thought up for the trash pile by the back door.

mowron: a person of limited intelligence. "That Bubba is a mowron. I ast him had he ever heard of Einstein and he said wasn't that some kind of a beer mug."

druthers: wishes. "If I had my druthers we'd fish a little closer to the dam, Elrod. They just put them signs up to scare people anyway."

sport: why outdoorsmen have to work. "I could get a lot more hunting and fishing done if I didn't have to sport that bunch."

barn: metal balls between a wheel and axle. "I believe we done burnt out another trailer barn."

tad: the rise and fall of the sea. "Don't worry, Elrod. We'll float off this alligator nest as soon as the tad comes in."

snuk: past tense of *sneak*. "I ain't mad because Bubba Junior snuk Beuletta out the house last night. I'm mad because he brung her back."

chew backey: popular tobacco product.

high mountain: phrase which expresses a dearth of something. "Cut me a plug, Elrod. High mountain chew backey."

tell you say: used to express surprise upon hearing an unlikely statement. "Bubba's going courting when he could be hunting with us? Tell you say."

waddermillon: large, juicy summer fruit that grows throughout the South.

live well: what an outdoorsman does in the South, and I'm not line!

Other Books from
August House Publishers

White Wolf Woman
and Other Native American Transformation Myths
Teresa Pijoan explores the common spirit which binds together
all forms of life through more than 40 transformation myths.

Hardback ISBN 0-87483-201-2
Paperback ISBN 0-87483-200-4

American Indians'
Kitchen-Table Stories
Contemporary Conversations with Cherokee, Sioux,
Hopi, Osage, Navajo, Zuni, and Members of Other Nations
Keith Cunningham collects more than 200 narratives
from conversations with contemporary Native American storytellers.

Hardback ISBN 0-87483-203-9
Paperback ISBN 0-87483-202-0

Rachel the Clever
and Other Jewish Folktales
Forty-six tales brought to America by immigrants from
countries and regions as diverse as the stories.
Collected and retold by Josepha Sherman.

Hardback ISBN 0-87483-306-X
Paperback ISBN 0-87483-307-8

African-American Folktales
Stories from the black oral tradition that transcend color and culture
collected and edited by Richard and Judy Dockrey Young.

Hardback ISBN 0-87483-308-6
Paperback ISBN 0-87483-309-4

August House Publishers
P.O. Box 3223, Little Rock, Arkansas 72203
1-800-284-8784